GRATITUDE

Giving Thanks in Life's Ups and Downs

8 STUDIES FOR INDIVIDUALS OR GROUPS

LifeGuide®
BIBLE STUDIES

DALE AND SANDY LARSEN

ivp

An imprint of InterVarsity Press
Downers Grove, Illinois

InterVarsity Press
P.O. Box 1400, Downers Grove, IL 60515-1426
ivpress.com
email@ivpress.com

InterVarsity Press® is the book-publishing division of InterVarsity Christian Fellowship/USA®, a movement of students and faculty active on campus at hundreds of universities, colleges, and schools of nursing in the United States of America, and a member movement of the International Fellowship of Evangelical Students. For information about local and regional activities, visit intervarsity.org.

Cover design and image composite: David Fassett
Interior design: Jeanna Wiggins
Image: sky lanterns: © ImpossiAble / Moment / Getty Images

ISBN 978-0-8308-3162-3 (print)
ISBN 978-0-8308-3163-0 (digital)

Printed in the United States of America ♾

InterVarsity Press is committed to ecological stewardship and to the conservation of natural resources in all our operations. This book was printed using sustainably sourced paper.

P *25 24 23 22 21 20 19 18 17 16 15 14 13 12 11 10 9 8 7*

Y *40 39 38 37 36 35 34 33 32 31 30 29 28 27 26*

CONTENTS

GETTING THE MOST OUT OF *GRATITUDE*

"I'm alive."

"People don't snitch on me."

"The staff here treat us well."

"I've learned to stand up for myself."

Inmates at our county jail made those responses when they were asked during a Bible study, "What do you have to be grateful for?" They put us to shame by their willingness to "give thanks in all circumstances; for this is God's will for you in Christ Jesus" (1 Thessalonians 5:18).

On the other hand, we'd had a difficult year.

The Polar Vortex of 2019 clobbered us with nonstop snow, brutal winds, and -30 degree temperature. That's -30 real degrees, never mind the wind chill. Our refrigerator quit, and for a week the Polar Vortex was our refrigerator—or rather freezer—as we set food outdoors in critter-proof containers. Both of us battled expensive health issues. To help with finances, Sandy became a substitute paraprofessional in the school system. She got knocked down on a playground by a herd of stampeding first graders and was laid up for several weeks. Dale needed cataract surgery. Our car had persistent problems.

As freelance writers we wanted and needed to generate more writing projects. Sandy—feeling self-conscious about using a cane during her recovery—had coffee with a friend and wondered out loud about possible topics for a new IVP LifeGuide Bible study.

Her friend suggested, "How about gratitude?"

Well now. Gratitude was not a topic that jumped to the foreground. Griping had become too much of a habit. With effort we put griping aside (most of the time) and began to explore gratitude to God.

This Bible study had barely gotten underway when the Covid-19 pandemic shut down much of the nation. As we write, churches, schools, and most businesses remain closed. No group gatherings. The "elbow bump" greeting has morphed into "stay at least six feet apart and wave." A surreal atmosphere has descended on our community.

Fortunately we work at home, so that didn't change. What has changed is that the unforeseen has happened. Our gratitude to God has started climbing again.

The window over our desk looks out on our quiet neighborhood street. We see more people than usual. People are out on the sidewalks and in their front yards much more than before. When strangers wave and ask each other, "How are you doing?" it means more than the typical trite "How are you?" We now know the names and some life stories of neighbors we'd barely spoken to before. We call and email people more than usual.

We have become more intensely aware, not only of the Lord and his care for us, but of people around us, their physical and spiritual needs, what they have to offer our community. We thank God for technology that enables our church family to continue to have "virtual corporate" worship and to meet in small groups. With a third of our city employed in health care, we are deeply grateful for those on the risky front lines of the virus.

Nobody likes a crisis, and nobody in the world likes the health crisis the world has gone through with Covid-19. Yet this study guide on gratitude has come out of that crisis. Whatever the global situation or your own personal situation as you pick up this book, we pray that your gratitude to God in Christ will grow because of it.

SUGGESTIONS FOR INDIVIDUAL STUDY

1. As you begin each study, pray that God will speak to you through his Word.

2. Read the introduction to the study and respond to the personal reflection question or exercise. This is designed to help you focus on God and on the theme of the study.

3. Each study deals with a particular passage—so that you can delve into the author's meaning in that context. Read and reread the passage to be studied. The questions are written using the language of the New International Version, so you may wish to use that version of the Bible. The New Revised Standard Version is also recommended.

4. This is an inductive Bible study, designed to help you discover for yourself what Scripture is saying. The study includes three types of questions. *Observation* questions ask about the basic facts: who, what, when, where, and how. *Interpretation* questions delve into the meaning of the passage. *Application* questions help you discover the implications of the text for growing in Christ. These three keys unlock the treasures of Scripture.

Write your answers to the questions in the spaces provided or in a personal journal. Writing can bring clarity and deeper understanding of yourself and of God's Word.

5. It might be good to have a Bible dictionary handy. Use it to look up any unfamiliar words, names, or places.

6. Use the prayer suggestion to guide you in thanking God for what you have learned and to pray about the applications that have come to mind.

7. You may want to go on to the suggestion under "Now or Later," or you may want to use that idea for your next study.

SUGGESTIONS FOR MEMBERS OF A GROUP STUDY

1. Come to the study prepared. Follow the suggestions for individual study mentioned above. You will find that careful preparation will greatly enrich your time spent in group discussion.

2. Be willing to participate in the discussion. The leader of your group will not be lecturing. Instead, he or she will be encouraging the members of the group to discuss what they have learned. The leader will be asking the questions that are found in this guide.

3. Stick to the topic being discussed. Your answers should be based on the verses which are the focus of the discussion and not on outside authorities such as commentaries or speakers. These studies focus on a particular passage of Scripture. Only rarely should you refer to other portions of the Bible. This allows for everyone to participate in in-depth study on equal ground.

4. Be sensitive to the other members of the group. Listen attentively when they describe what they have learned. You may be surprised by their insights! Each question assumes a variety of answers. Many questions do not have "right" answers, particularly questions that aim at meaning or application. Instead the questions push us to explore the passage more thoroughly.

When possible, link what you say to the comments of others. Also, be affirming whenever you can. This will encourage some of the more hesitant members of the group to participate.

5. Be careful not to dominate the discussion. We are sometimes so eager to express our thoughts that we leave too little opportunity for others to respond. By all means participate! But allow others to also.

6. Expect God to teach you through the passage being discussed and through the other members of the group. Pray that you will have an enjoyable and profitable time together, but also that as a result of the study you will find ways that you can take action individually and/or as a group.

7. Remember that anything said in the group is considered confidential and should not be discussed outside the group unless specific permission is given to do so.

8. If you are the group leader, you will find additional suggestions at the back of the guide.

ONE

GRATITUDE GOES BOTH WAYS

Philippians 4:10-20

In her Ask Amy advice column, Amy Dickinson wonders if our society has a "gratitude deficit." Recipients of wedding gifts, birthday gifts, and Christmas gifts fail to send thank-you notes or even thank-you texts or phone calls. Amy wonders, "Do people lack the emotional tools to understand the connection between receiving something (a gift, a kindness, a nice gesture) and expressing their thanks? Can people not comprehend the joy of connection when they close the loop by saying, 'Thank you'?"*

Even in a Roman prison, the apostle Paul had no gratitude deficit. He closed the loop with a warm letter to the Christians of Philippi thanking them for their generous gift and encouraging them in their faith.

Group Discussion. How is your gratitude affected when you receive a gift (whether material items, physical help, a special favor, or anything else) when it is given to you by

- a close friend?
- a family member?
- someone in less fortunate circumstances than you?
- your church?
- an anonymous donor?

What do you think makes the difference, if there is one?

Personal Reflection. How do you react when someone thanks you for a gift? Consider how you respond both inwardly (feelings) and outwardly (words and actions).

The church in Philippi was planted after Paul had a vision of a Macedonian man begging him, "Come over to Macedonia and help us" (Acts 16:9). Now he is imprisoned, probably in Rome (see Philippians 1:12-14). His colleague Epaphroditus has delivered generous gifts to Paul from the Philippian Christians. Paul writes to thank them and to encourage them in their faith. *Read Philippians 4:10-20.*

1. What words or phrases would you use to describe Paul's outlook on life in this passage?

2. When have you shared Paul's outlook on life, or something like it, and why?

3. Apparently there had been a gap in the Philippians' material support for Paul (vv. 10-11). What is his attitude toward this interruption?

4. Paul said that he could be content in all extremities of circumstances, good and bad. How does he let us in on his "secret" of contentment (vv. 12-13)?

5. In verse 14, Paul returns to his gratitude for the Philippians. How have they proved themselves faithful supporters of Paul's ministry (vv. 14-16)?

6. Paul tells the Philippian Christians, "Not that I desire your gifts; what I desire is that more be credited to your account" (v. 17). What do you think he means by "credited to your account"?

7. Paul describes the Philippians' gifts in almost effusive terms (v. 18). When have you thanked someone in terms like these, and why?

8. Why can the Philippians' gift to Paul also be considered "a fragrant offering, an acceptable sacrifice, pleasing to God" (v. 18)?

9. Paul brings his letter toward its close with profound assurance of God's provision not only for him but also for his letter's recipients (vv. 19-20). How might his assurance have affected the Philippian church?

10. When you have given generously and sacrificially, whether of material things or in other ways, how has the gratitude of others affected you?

11. Whom can you bless by expressing your gratitude, even if it is overdue? Make plans to express your thanks to that person (or group) this week. You might wish to use Paul's expression of thanks as a guide.

Pray that expressing sincere thanks, both to other people and to the Lord, will become your regular habit.

NOW OR LATER

Study Philippians 1:1-10, in which Paul tells the Philippian Christians, "I thank my God every time I remember you," expresses confidence of God's working in their lives, and offers heartfelt prayers for their growth in Christ.

---

*Amy Dickinson, "Ingratitude Has Reached Epidemic Proportions," ArcaMax, October 1, 2019, www.arcamax.com/healthandspirit/lifeadvice/askamy/s-2279043?fs.

TWO

THE GREAT GRATITUDE FADE-OUT

Deuteronomy 8:6-18

The phrase "Lest we forget" appears on war memorials and other commemorations of those who have sacrificed their lives for a cause. The words caution us not to let the dead slip from our memories. In Rudyard Kipling's 1897 poem "Recessional," the recurring phrase warned the British Empire to put faith in the "Judge of the Nations" rather than in their own imperial power.

The origin of the phrase "lest we forget" goes back further than the last couple of centuries. As the Israelites were on the verge of entering the fruitful promised land of Canaan, God cautioned them through Moses, "Take care lest you forget the LORD your God" (Deuteronomy 8:11 ESV).

Group Discussion. What are some examples of great gifts that people take for granted?

Personal Reflection. When have you realized that you did not fully appreciate a gift, whether material or otherwise? What did you do when you realized this?

When Jacob learned that his son Joseph had risen to prominence in Egypt, Jacob and his extended family went to Egypt to be reunited and to escape famine. The death of Joseph and a new pharaoh changed everything, and the Israelites became the Egyptians' slaves. The Egyptians "made their lives bitter with harsh labor in brick and mortar and with all kinds of work in the fields" (Exodus 1:14). Years later they still "groaned in their slavery and cried out, and their cry for help because of their slavery went up to God. God heard their groaning and he remembered his covenant with Abraham, with Isaac and with Jacob. So God looked on the Israelites and was concerned about them" (Exodus 2:23-25). God sent Moses to lead Israel out of Egypt and into the promised land of Canaan. *Read Deuteronomy 8:6-18.*

1. The book of Deuteronomy is Moses' farewell address to the Israelites as they are on the verge of entering the land of promise. Moses reviews the history of their desert wanderings and reiterates the laws God has given them. According to this passage, what will their coming life in this "good land" be like?

2. After all the blessings God has given the Israelites and the additional blessings he promises to give them, why should God need to say, "Be careful that you do not forget the LORD your God" (v. 11)?

3. How does such ungrateful forgetfulness contrast with Paul's attitude in study one (Philippians 4:10-20)?

4. The Israelites were hardly unique. Why do you think people in general so quickly forget God?

5. When the Israelites lost faith in God, he declared that none of the original population who left Egypt would enter Canaan, with very few exceptions (Numbers 14:20-35). If those about to enter Canaan are an entirely new generation, how can they *remember* the Lord "who brought you out of Egypt, out of the land of slavery" (v. 14)?

6. Why should the struggles of verses 15-16 motivate the Israelites to continue to remember and be grateful to the Lord?

7. Once the Israelites are established in the land, with what will they be tempted to replace gratitude to God (vv. 14, 17)?

8. In what areas of your life do you face the same temptation?

9. Consider the admonition of verse 18. What are some practical ways you can remind yourself that all you have and all you accomplish come from God's generosity to you?

10. What is one way you will remind yourself of that truth this week?

Pray that you will continue (or begin) to depend fully on the Lord and not on your own strength and abilities.

NOW OR LATER

Study Luke 17:11-19, an example of the contrast between gratitude and ingratitude in the face of one of Jesus' miracles.

THREE

A GRATEFUL FELLOWSHIP

Colossians 3:12-17

A **testimonial dinner.** A medal presentation. A volunteer appreciation event. Society has many occasions to gather in honor of someone and say "thanks for a job well done." Sometimes the recipient is not quite ready for the award. When all-time leading harness-racing driver John Campbell was honored with a lifetime achievement award at age fifty-eight, he responded, "Lifetime achievement? I've got news for you, I'm not done, on or off the track."*

When Christian believers gather to give thanks to God, it is not only for the completed work of Christ on the cross; it is also for what God is continuing to do in our lives. He is not finished with us! Every time we meet together, we thank him for what he has done and for what he is doing and will do for us.

Group Discussion. What would you say is the basis for Christian fellowship? If your answer is only a brief phrase, try to expand on your answer.

Personal Reflection. Consider Christian fellowships you have been a part of: churches, Bible studies, ministry endeavors, and others. Which one are you most grateful for, and why?

Paul's associate Epaphras had brought the gospel to the city of Colossae in Asia Minor (Colossians 1:7). Now Paul writes the Colossian Christians a warm personal letter. He exalts Christ as preeminent and warns against false teaching that undermines the supremacy of Christ. *Read Colossians 3:12-17.*

1. "Therefore" (v. 12) refers to Paul's counsel in verses 1-11 for the Colossians to set their minds on Christ, put off their old manner of life, and put on Christlikeness. How do the qualities named in verses 12-17 reflect the character of Christ?

2. Why would an underlying sense of thankfulness to the Lord—for both spiritual and temporal blessings—give rise to the attitudes and behavior of verses 12-14?

3. When has being thankful for your own forgiveness in Christ led you to forgive someone else?

4. Consider a church fellowship that lives in accordance with verses 12-14. How would worshiping in such a fellowship deepen your gratitude to God?

5. Peace and thankfulness are presented here as natural accompaniments to each other (v. 15). Why is a heart ruled by the peace of Christ also a thankful heart?

6. Paul assumes that when the Colossian Christians meet together, they will teach and admonish one another with wisdom (v. 16). *Teach* implies positive instruction, while *admonish* implies warning against what is wrong. When have you been grateful for other believers' teaching?

7. When have you been grateful for other believers' admonishment?

8. Paul also assumes that the Colossian Christians will sing together with gratitude in their hearts (v. 16). How does singing with other believers intensify your thankfulness to the Lord?

9. "Whatever you do," Paul says, whether words or actions, do it in the name of Jesus, with thankfulness to God (v. 17). How does gratefulness to the Lord encourage you to bring *all* areas of your life under the name of the Lord Jesus?

10. Consider your relationships with other believers, especially those of your immediate fellowship. What parts of your life with them are *not* under the authority of Christ—where you often do not act or speak in ways that honor his name? Weigh your attitude as well as your overt words and actions.

11. What is one way you will change your attitudes and behavior toward other believers this week, so that you can truly say you are acting in Jesus' name?

Thank God for your fellowship of believers. Pray that you will faithfully foster an attitude of thankfulness together.

NOW OR LATER

Study Romans 15:1-13, in which Paul urges believers to accept each other in order to bring praise to God.

---

*"Campbell Still Passionate for Meadowlands Pace," HarnessRacing.com, July 10, 2013, www.harnessracing.com/news/main/campbellstillpassionateformeadow landspace.

FOUR

CORRECTED AND THANKFUL

Hebrews 12:4-13

We **told a friend that** we had moved into Sandy's childhood home. Our friend asked Sandy, "Do you send yourself to your room?"

When a child misbehaves, parents often order, "Go to your room!" The order can backfire. If the room is full of books, toys, and games, the kid may love being sent there. At other times the child emerges with an improved attitude. Whatever form discipline takes, and whether it works or not, all well-meaning parents use it to correct and train their children toward better behavior.

God our heavenly Father is wiser than any human parent about how to discipline us. He has only our good at heart.

Group Discussion. Why do children usually resent being disciplined by their parents?

Personal Reflection. What forms do you think God's discipline takes?

The unknown author of Hebrews wrote to Christians who were converts from Judaism and who were very familiar with Jewish law and practices. The writer and the recipients apparently knew each other (see Hebrews 13:19, 23). The letter's theme is the supremacy of Christ and his fulfillment of all the Old Testament sacrifices. The writer urges the recipients, who are under persecution, to throw off sin and persevere in the Christian life, focusing on Jesus. Then comes the admonition to submit to God's discipline. *Read Hebrews 12:4-13.*

1. According to this passage, how does God's discipline demonstrate that we are his children?

2. The writer quotes Proverbs 3:11-12 as a "word of encouragement" (v. 5). In what sense could such advice be considered encouraging?

3. How is a child's attitude toward discipline changed by the understanding that the discipline is motivated by love?

4. What forms might God's discipline take in our lives?

5. When we feel that God is making our lives difficult and we are not sure why, how can this passage help us understand what is happening? See especially verses 10-11.

6. When we were disciplined as children, we almost always knew why. The discipline was an immediate consequence of our disobedience. Do you think that we always recognize the reasons for God's discipline at the time? Think of examples from your own experience.

7. This passage makes it clear that the Lord lovingly corrects his children. Why should we be grateful for this discipline?

8. Consider how God has disciplined you in the past. How did your response compare to the "harvest of righteousness and peace" that Hebrews describes as the result of discipline (v. 11)?

9. Examining your own life, where and how do you need to "strengthen your feeble arms and weak knees" and "make level paths for your feet" as the writer of Hebrews admonishes (vv. 12-13)?

10. How will you express gratitude to the Lord for his loving correction, even if it is difficult?

Pray that you will recognize and submit to the Lord's loving discipline. Thank him for caring enough to correct your attitudes and behavior.

NOW OR LATER

Study Psalm 32, an example of prayer after God's severe discipline for sin.

Study the book of Jonah, especially chapter 2, to see a dramatic example of repentance after discipline.

FIVE

GRATEFUL FOR GOD'S GRACE

Ephesians 1:3-14

One Thanksgiving our local newspaper carried an ad from a daycare center naming things for which the children were thankful. The responses were sweet, such as "my mommy and daddy," "my bear," "my blanket." The daycare center, however, issued a disclaimer. Because being thankful was too hard a concept for these little ones to grasp, the children were asked instead, "What makes you happy?"

What an odd take on thanksgiving! There is all the difference in the world between being happy and being thankful. Happiness turns inward on subjective feeling; thankfulness turns outward toward the giver of the gift for which we are thankful. The apostle Paul did not just feel happy when he considered God's mercy; he overflowed with thanksgiving to his merciful God.

Group Discussion. If you were asked what a *blessing* is, how would you respond?

Personal Reflection. What are some ways that you regularly thank God for his mercy toward you? Consider both words and actions.

Acts 19 relates Paul's history with the church in Ephesus, a strategic city located at a crossroads of major trade routes in what is now Turkey. Paul stayed in Ephesus two years, preaching Christ in the synagogue and later in a lecture hall. God performed miracles through Paul, and sorcerers were converted to Christ. But tradespeople who made pagan images became distressed at their loss of trade and incited a riot against Paul. After things quieted down, Paul set off for Macedonia. *Read Ephesians 1:3-14.*

1. In the original Greek, verses 3-14 are all one sentence, as though Paul got going with his praise and couldn't stop. Paul writes that God has "blessed us in the heavenly realms with every spiritual blessing in Christ" (v. 3). He then goes on to name some of these blessings. Which of these blessings from God would you consider "past," which ones "present," and which ones "future"? There may be some overlap.

2. Which of the blessings in verses 3-14 involve God the Father?

3. Which blessings involve Christ?

4. Which blessings involve the Holy Spirit?

5. Christ has "blessed us in the heavenly realms" (v. 3). What difference does it make that our blessings are not merely earthly but heavenly?

6. What new relationship do we have with God the Father, and how did it come about (vv. 4-6)?

7. In order to be sincerely grateful for the gifts named in verses 7-10, what must we *not* believe about ourselves?

8. God's plan is "to bring unity to all things in heaven and on earth under Christ" (v. 10). Identify some things that are broken or fragmented now that you long to see unified under Christ.

9. What reasons do you find in verses 11-14 to be grateful to God?

10. Like Paul, we have all been overwhelmed with gratitude for the blessings named in this Scripture passage. It would be too difficult to say which ones inspire the most gratitude. But for which of these blessings have you been especially grateful *lately*?

11. Write out a prayer of thanks to the Lord expressing why you have been especially grateful for those blessings lately.

Thank God for lavishing on you his many gifts of mercy in Christ. Pray that you will show something of the same mercy toward others.

NOW OR LATER

Study 1 Timothy 1:12-17, in which Paul recalls his former life of opposing Christ and thanks Christ for his mercy.

Recall how you first "heard the message of truth, the gospel of your salvation" (Ephesians 1:13), including where and from whom you learned it. If possible, communicate with the person or people who first told you the gospel. Tell them how grateful you are that they faithfully passed along the message. Even if you cannot contact them, spend extra time thanking the Lord for them. Resolve to do for others what they did for you.

SIX

GLAD TO TAKE HEAT

1 Peter 4:12-19

Matthew Meyer was on mile sixteen of the 2019 Boston Marathon, and his exhausted body wanted to drop out. Instead of quitting, he tried something suggested by other marathoners: he made mile sixteen a "gratitude mile." As he ran that mile, he thought about all the things he was grateful for. His strength was renewed, and he finished the race. Meyer later explained, "Taking a mile to think about what you are thankful for helps you shift your mindset and get past midrun slump."*

Whether or not we are marathoners, Christians also experience "midrun slump." Life gets too tough for us. We wonder how we can continue to take the heat and persevere. While a marathoner's gratitude mile may be only an exercise in emotional self-talk, our gratitude to the Lord can get us past our midrun slump and give us energy to finish the race.

Group Discussion. What discourages Christians in their faith, and what reenergizes them?

Personal Reflection. When have you been discouraged and even wanted to quit the Christian life, and what has helped you get past that point?

First Peter is a general letter to followers of Christ scattered throughout the Roman Empire; by extension, it is directed to all Christians scattered throughout the world. Peter writes about our hope, the preeminence of Christ, and how we should live together in harmony. In 1 Peter 3:8-9 he introduces the theme of suffering with and for Christ. Peter's words show his spiritual maturity, for at first he had refused to believe that Christ would suffer at all (Matthew 16:21-22). *Read 1 Peter 4:12-19.*

1. How does Peter's advice here run radically counter to people's usual perception of suffering?

2. Why might Christians especially think that it is "strange" if they suffer (v. 12)?

3. What specific reasons does Peter offer for being glad in the midst of suffering (vv. 13-16)?

4. In what sense do believers "participate in the sufferings of Christ" (v. 13)?

5. In what ways have you been "insulted because of the name of Christ" (v. 14)?

6. How have you experienced God's blessing for being insulted for Christ?

7. If Christ has taken God's judgment for sin onto himself, what can Peter mean by "it is time for judgment to begin with God's household" (vv. 17-18)?

8. If you seldom or never take any heat for being a Christian, what might you conclude about your life?

9. What hope does verse 19 offer a believer who is suffering for Christ?

10. How does choosing to thank and praise God help strengthen Christians in the midst of struggles?

11. Taking verse 19 as your model, as you commit yourself to your faithful Creator, how will you "continue to do good" this week?

Pray for persecuted Christians worldwide and in your own area, especially those you know personally. Pray as 1 Peter 4:19 directs, committing yourself to your Creator, who remains steadfastly faithful to you.

NOW OR LATER

Study Peter's extended treatment of suffering in 1 Peter 3:8–4:11, which leads up to this session's Scripture passage.

Think of people you know who are undergoing hardship for their faith in Christ. Plan ways to encourage them by letting them know you are praying for them and if possible asking how you can be of help.

---

*Matthew Meyer, "When the Going Gets Tough, Gratitude Keeps You Going," *Runner's World* 55, no. 1 (2020): 18-20.

SEVEN

INTO THE UNKNOWN WITH GRATITUDE

2 Chronicles 20:1-30

When we email a request for someone to do something for us, we routinely close with "Thank you in advance." Lately we have learned that some people find this closing presumptuous. It seems that "Thank you in advance" puts the recipient under pressure; it demands a yes even if the recipient would rather say no. A more polite closing is a "call to action," such as "Do you think you'll have time to . . . ?" or the simple statement "I appreciate your help with . . ."*

King Jehoshaphat did not worry about being presumptuous with the Lord when Judah was threatened with invasion by enemy forces. The king sent out people ahead of his army to loudly thank the Lord for victory *in advance*. Jehoshaphat was confident that God would not say, "Sorry, can't help you with that."

Group Discussion. How does thanking God help us face the unknown?

Personal Reflection. When have you thanked God for an answer to prayer you had not yet seen? What made you confident of God's answer?

King Jehoshaphat's twenty-five-year reign in ninth-century BC Judah was marked by military power, wealth, and spiritual reform, though tainted with unwise alliances. He sent out teachers to instruct the people in God's law, took steps toward ridding Judah of idolatry, and cautioned judges to settle disputes fairly. In his day the long-running warfare between Judah and Israel was ended; however, nearby nations still threatened invasion. *Read 2 Chronicles 20:1-19.*

1. Consider the threat to Judah and the response of the people and Jehoshaphat (vv. 1-4). What clues do they give you about the spiritual mood in Judah at that time?

2. In his prayer (vv. 6-12), what does Jehoshaphat "remind" God about concerning God's character and past dealings with his people?

3. Even if Jehoshaphat does not overtly thank the Lord in his prayer, how does his prayer imply gratitude to God?

4. Jehoshaphat draws strength from looking back to God's saving history with his people. As you look back at your own life, where are you especially thankful for God's faithfulness to you?

5. When and why have you prayed something similar to what Jehoshaphat prayed in verse 12?

6. Why would Jahaziel's prophecy (vv. 14-17) produce the responses of verses 18-19?

7. *Read 2 Chronicles 20:20-30.* Picture the prayer force who leads the charge against the enemy. What might you expect them to be singing or saying, and what do they say instead?

8. What were the results of Jehoshaphat's unusual strategy?

9. What makes it possible for believers to express gratitude to God for answers to prayer we have not yet seen?

10. "Do not be afraid; do not be discouraged. Go out to face them tomorrow, and the LORD will be with you" (v. 17). In what situation do you need to hear those words right now, perhaps with a different timeline than "tomorrow"?

11. How will you thank God for what he will do for you in that situation, even though you cannot yet see his answer?

"We do not know what to do, but our eyes are on you." Thank God for what he is going to accomplish on your behalf. Actively expect his answers. Pray that you will be delivered from fear and discouragement and will "stand firm and see the deliverance the LORD will give you."

NOW OR LATER

For a similar, earlier occasion of the Lord granting victory without a battle, study Judges 7, in which Gideon's three-hundred-man army encounters the Midianites. Note how "each man held his position" while the Midianites fled (Judges 7:21).

For a similar, later occasion of the Lord granting victory without a battle, study 2 Kings 18–19, Assyria's siege of Jerusalem under King Hezekiah. The event is also recorded in Isaiah 36–37 and more briefly in 2 Chronicles 32:1-23.

---

*Karen Hertzberg, "5 Alternative Ways to Say 'Thank You in Advance,'" Grammarly, updated September 4, 2017, www.grammarly.com/blog/thank-you-in-advance.

EIGHT

UNENDING THANKS

Psalm 107

In his 1962 book *Six Crises,* Richard M. Nixon advised staying vigilant in the wake of a crisis. He wrote, "The easiest period in a crisis situation is actually the battle itself. The most difficult is the period of indecision—whether to fight or run away. And the most dangerous period is the aftermath. It is then, with all his resources spent and his guard down, that an individual must watch out for dulled reactions and faulty judgment."*

Psalm 107 draws several dramatic pictures of people in extreme danger. Whether the people involved had an emotional letdown when the danger was past, we do not know. We do know that in the aftermath of each crisis, the psalm writer urged the people to give thanks to the Lord for his unfailing love.

Group Discussion. What keeps people thankful to God over the long haul?

Personal Reflection. When have you come through a crisis and been overwhelmed with thankfulness to the Lord? How did you express that thanks?

After a general call for the "redeemed" to give thanks to the Lord and tell their story in verses 1-3, Psalm 107 recounts several situations in which the Lord rescued people who were in desperate need. Each account ends with a call to give thanks. We are not told the time or location of these events; at some points they resemble the Israelites' exodus from Egypt. While the situations are literal, they can also stand as metaphors for other physical or spiritual crises. *Read Psalm 107:1-9.*

1. What state did these people reach before they "cried out to the LORD in their trouble" (v. 6)?

2. How did the Lord respond to the desperate wanderers (vv. 6-9)?

3. When has the Lord brought you to a safe home, whether literally or spiritually (or both)?

4. *Read Psalm 107:10-16.* Here we are told the reason for the prisoners' suffering. Why were they in this desperate situation?

5. Consider some "iron chains," "gates of bronze," and "bars of iron" that bind people today. What hope does this passage offer that would lead to giving thanks?

6. *Read Psalm 107:17-22.* In the Bible *fools* (v. 17) are people who are morally rather than mentally deficient. These fools brought an affliction on themselves that resulted in lethal illness. How could the Lord's word rescue them from death?

7. *Read Psalm 107:23-32.* Trace the stages in the sailors' story from their first appreciation of God's creation to their coming safely into harbor. If you had been on that ship, how would you have felt at each stage of the journey?

8. Verses 6, 13, 19, and 28 are identical or almost identical. So are verses 8, 15, 21, and 31. What does the writer of the psalm emphasize by such repetition?

9. *Read Psalm 107:33-43.* Here people's life conditions ebb and flow, but there is no explanation of why, except that their circumstances were all under God's control. What makes the difference between two different reactions to these events (v. 42)?

10. We would expect Psalm 107 to conclude with a final call for gratitude. Instead it ends with a summons to pay attention to these things and consider the great love of the Lord (v. 43). How have difficulties in your own life taught you more about the Lord's love for you?

11. Looking back over this entire study guide on gratitude, what changes have you seen in your own sense of thankfulness toward God?

12. What changes in your sense of thankfulness toward God would you still like to see?

Thank God for hard times and for what he has shown you about himself and about yourself through those times.

NOW OR LATER

Recall difficulties in your life through which the Lord showed you his faithfulness and care. Perhaps some of the struggles were of your own making, while others were simply common circumstances of human life. Using Psalm 107 as a model, write your own psalm of thanksgiving to the Lord. It doesn't have to be as lengthy as Psalm 107; however, as you recall more and more events from your life, it may turn out to be even longer!

---

*Richard M. Nixon, *Six Crises* (Garden City, NY: Doubleday, 1962), xv.

LEADER'S NOTES

My grace is sufficient for you.

2 CORINTHIANS 12:9

Leading a Bible discussion can be an enjoyable and rewarding experience. But it can also be *scary*—especially if you've never done it before. If this is your feeling, you're in good company. When God asked Moses to lead the Israelites out of Egypt, he replied, "O Lord, please send someone else to do it" (Exodus 4:13). It was the same with Solomon, Jeremiah, and Timothy, but God helped these people in spite of their weaknesses, and he will help you as well.

You don't need to be an expert on the Bible or a trained teacher to lead a Bible discussion. The idea behind these inductive studies is that the leader guides group members to discover for themselves what the Bible has to say. This method of learning will allow group members to remember much more of what is said than a lecture would.

These studies are designed to be led easily. As a matter of fact, the flow of questions through the passage from observation to interpretation to application is so natural that you may feel that the studies lead themselves. This study guide is also flexible. You can use it with a variety of groups—student, professional, neighborhood, or church groups. Each study takes forty-five to sixty minutes in a group setting.

There are some important facts to know about group dynamics and encouraging discussion. The suggestions listed below should enable you to effectively and enjoyably fulfill your role as leader.

PREPARING FOR THE STUDY

1. Ask God to help you understand and apply the passage in your own life. Unless this happens, you will not be prepared to lead others. Pray

too for the various members of the group. Ask God to open your hearts to the message of his Word and motivate you to action.

2. Read the introduction to the entire guide to get an overview of the entire book and the issues which will be explored.

3. As you begin each study, read and reread the assigned Bible passage to familiarize yourself with it.

4. This study guide is based on the New International Version of the Bible. It will help you and the group if you use this translation as the basis for your study and discussion.

5. Carefully work through each question in the study. Spend time in meditation and reflection as you consider how to respond.

6. Write your thoughts and responses in the space provided in the study guide. This will help you to express your understanding of the passage clearly.

7. It might help to have a Bible dictionary handy. Use it to look up any unfamiliar words, names, or places. (For additional help on how to study a passage, see chapter five of *How to Lead a LifeGuide Bible Study,* InterVarsity Press.)

8. Consider how you can apply the Scripture to your life. Remember that the group will follow your lead in responding to the studies. They will not go any deeper than you do.

9. Once you have finished your own study of the passage, familiarize yourself with the leader's notes for the study you are leading. These are designed to help you in several ways. First, they tell you the purpose the study guide author had in mind when writing the study. Take time to think through how the study questions work together to accomplish that purpose. Second, the notes provide you with additional background information or suggestions on group dynamics for various questions. This information can be useful when people have difficulty understanding or answering a question. Third, the leader's notes can alert you to potential problems you may encounter during the study.

10. If you wish to remind yourself of anything mentioned in the leader's notes, make a note to yourself below that question in the study.

LEADING THE STUDY

1. Begin the study on time. Open with prayer, asking God to help the group to understand and apply the passage.

2. Be sure that everyone in your group has a study guide. Encourage the group to prepare beforehand for each discussion by reading the introduction to the guide and by working through the questions in the study.

3. At the beginning of your first time together, explain that these studies are meant to be discussions, not lectures. Encourage the members of the group to participate. However, do not put pressure on those who may be hesitant to speak during the first few sessions. You may want to suggest the following guidelines to your group.

- Stick to the topic being discussed.
- Your responses should be based on the verses which are the focus of the discussion and not on outside authorities such as commentaries or speakers.
- These studies focus on a particular passage of Scripture. Only rarely should you refer to other portions of the Bible. This allows for everyone to participate in in-depth study on equal ground.
- Anything said in the group is considered confidential and will not be discussed outside the group unless specific permission is given to do so.
- We will listen attentively to each other and provide time for each person present to talk.
- We will pray for each other.

4. Have a group member read the introduction at the beginning of the discussion.

5. Every session begins with a group discussion question. The question or activity is meant to be used before the passage is read. The question introduces the theme of the study and encourages group members to begin to open up. Encourage as many members as possible to participate, and be ready to get the discussion going with your own response.

This section is designed to reveal where our thoughts or feelings need to be transformed by Scripture. That is why it is especially important not to read the passage before the discussion question is asked. The passage will tend to color the honest reactions people would otherwise give because they are, of course, supposed to think the way the Bible does.

You may want to supplement the group discussion question with an icebreaker to help people to get comfortable. See the community section of InterVarsity Press's *Small Group Idea Book* for more ideas.

You also might want to use the personal reflection question with your group. Either allow a time of silence for people to respond individually or discuss it together.

6. Have a group member (or members if the passage is long) read aloud the passage to be studied. Then give people several minutes to read the passage again silently so that they can take it all in.

7. Question 1 will generally be an overview question designed to briefly survey the passage. Encourage the group to look at the whole passage, but try to avoid getting sidetracked by questions or issues that will be addressed later in the study.

8. As you ask the questions, keep in mind that they are designed to be used just as they are written. You may simply read them aloud. Or you may prefer to express them in your own words.

There may be times when it is appropriate to deviate from the study guide. For example, a question may have already been answered. If so, move on to the next question. Or someone may raise an important question not covered in the guide. Take time to discuss it, but try to keep the group from going off on tangents.

9. Avoid answering your own questions. If necessary, repeat or rephrase them until they are clearly understood. Or point out something you read in the leader's notes to clarify the context or meaning. An eager group quickly becomes passive and silent if they think the leader will do most of the talking.

10. Don't be afraid of silence. People may need time to think about the question before formulating their answers.

11. Don't be content with just one answer. Ask, "What do the rest of you think?" or "Anything else?" until several people have given answers to the question.

12. Acknowledge all contributions. Try to be affirming whenever possible. Never reject an answer. If it is clearly off base, ask, "Which verse led you to that conclusion?" or again, "What do the rest of you think?"

13. Don't expect every answer to be addressed to you, even though this will probably happen at first. As group members become more at ease, they will begin to truly interact with each other. This is one sign of healthy discussion.

14. Don't be afraid of controversy. It can be very stimulating. If you don't resolve an issue completely, don't be frustrated. Move on and keep it in mind for later. A subsequent study may solve the problem.

15. Periodically summarize what the group has said about the passage. This helps to draw together the various ideas mentioned and gives continuity to the study. But don't preach.

16. At the end of the Bible discussion, you may want to allow group members a time of quiet to work on an idea under "Now or Later." Then discuss what you experienced. Or you may want to encourage group members to work on these ideas between meetings. Give an opportunity during the session for people to talk about what they are learning.

17. Conclude your time together with conversational prayer, adapting the prayer suggestion at the end of the study to your group. Ask for God's help in following through on the commitments you've made.

18. End on time.

Many more suggestions and helps are found in *How to Lead a LifeGuide Bible Study,* which is part of the LifeGuide Bible Study series.

COMPONENTS OF SMALL GROUPS

A healthy small group should do more than study the Bible. There are four components to consider as you structure your time together.

Nurture. Small groups help us to grow in our knowledge and love of God. Bible study is the key to making this happen and is the foundation of your small group.

Community. Small groups are a great place to develop deep friendships with other Christians. Allow time for informal interaction before and after each study. Plan activities and games that will help you get to know each other. Spend time having fun together—going on a picnic or cooking dinner together.

Worship and prayer. Your study will be enhanced by spending time praising God together in prayer or song. Pray for each other's needs—and keep track of how God is answering prayer in your group. Ask God to help you to apply what you are learning in your study.

Outreach. Reaching out to others can be a practical way of applying what you are learning, and it will keep your group from becoming self-focused. Host a series of evangelistic discussions for your friends or neighbors. Clean up the yard of an elderly friend. Serve at a soup kitchen together, or spend a day working on a Habitat house.

Many more suggestions and helps in each of these areas are found in *Small Group Idea Book.* Information on building a small group can be found in *Small Group Leaders' Handbook* and *The Big Book on Small Groups* (both from InterVarsity Press). Reading through one of these books would be worth your time.

STUDY 1. GRATITUDE GOES BOTH WAYS. PHILIPPIANS 4:10-20.

PURPOSE: To consider how gratitude blesses both the giver and the receiver of a gift.

Question 5. The Philippians' support followed Paul even after he left them and went to Thessalonica (Acts 17:1). Their ongoing support was unique among the Macedonian churches.

Question 6. The benefit the Philippians will receive is not necessarily material or financial but spiritual. They have invested in him and his ministry, and they will be spiritually rewarded, although Paul does not specify how.

Question 8. In Romans 12:1, Paul referred to the offering of our own bodies as "a living sacrifice, holy and pleasing to God—this is your true and proper worship." This offering imitates, however poorly, the sacrifice of Christ, who "loved us and gave himself up for us as a fragrant offering and sacrifice to God" (Ephesians 5:2).

STUDY 2. THE GREAT GRATITUDE FADE-OUT. DEUTERONOMY 8:6-18.

PURPOSE: To intentionally remember the Lord and honor him for what he has given us.

Question 3. Paul had a humble attitude of thankfulness for the generosity of the Lord and of the Philippian church. He could cope with all circumstances, not through his own strength but "through him who gives me strength" (Philippians 4:13).

Question 4. As we enjoy the benefits God has given us, we begin to focus on the benefits themselves and feel less dependent on the God who provides them. We also begin to assume that the good things we enjoy are things we have provided for ourselves. We are less thankful because we imagine that these are all things we deserve.

Question 5. No doubt the events of the exodus—the plagues, the Passover, the escape from Egypt, the miraculous crossing of the Red Sea—were told and retold during the desert wanderings. The new generation had grown up hearing the narrative of their God-directed history.

STUDY 3. A GRATEFUL FELLOWSHIP. COLOSSIANS 3:12-17.

PURPOSE: To encourage love for others out of gratitude for the Lord's love for us.

Question 5. The word translated *rule* (v. 15) literally means "to act as an umpire" and therefore "to arbitrate, decide." (See W. E. Vine, Merrill F. Unger, and William White Jr., "Rule," in *Vine's Complete Expository Dictionary of Old and New Testament Words* [Nashville: Thomas Nelson, 1996], 540.) A heart filled with the peace of Christ knows that it would be hopelessly lost without Christ and is profoundly grateful to him.

Question 8. Bible scholar and teacher John Stott, in his book about learning from the birds, points out the central place of joyous singing in Christian worship. "Temples, synagogues and mosques never resound with the exuberant praise of those who know their sins have been forgiven." We are irrepressible about this, Stott said. "It would be impossible to stop us singing." (John Stott, *The Birds Our Teachers* [Grand Rapids: Baker, 2001], 81-82.)

Question 9. To do everything in the name of Jesus means that "all of life is to be lived under the conscious authority of Christ and in active, thankful allegiance to his magnificent person" (A. Boyd Luter Jr., "Name," in *Dictionary of Paul and His Letters*, ed. Gerald F. Hawthorne and Ralph P. Martin [Downers Grove, IL: InterVarsity Press, 1993], para. 7205; accessed via *The Essential IVP Reference Collection* CD-ROM, 2003).

Question 10. Honestly consider faults such as gossip, criticism, undermining God-given authority, neglect of others' needs, or indifference to fellowship. We easily fall into these harmful patterns and don't realize how they damage our unity in Christ.

STUDY 4. CORRECTED AND THANKFUL. HEBREWS 12:4-13.

PURPOSE: To appreciate the loving parental discipline of our heavenly Father.

Question 1. Older Bible translations render *discipline* in verses 5-11 as *chastening* and *chastisement*; however, the connotation of the Greek word is closer to *instructing, training, education,* and *correction.* (See W. E. Vine, Merrill F. Unger, and William White Jr., "Chasten, Chastening, Chastise, Chastisement," in *Vine's Complete Expository Dictionary of Old and New Testament Words* [Nashville: Thomas Nelson, 1996], 97.) The exception is the word *chastens* in verse 6, part of a quote from the Greek translation of Proverbs 3:11-12. This word means "scourge"; it is what Pilate ordered done to Jesus (John 19:1). (See Vine, "Scourge," *Expository Dictionary*, 551.) Even if God's discipline of his children at times feels like scourging or flogging, it is never judicial punishment for sin. All of Hebrews insists that Christ has already taken onto himself the punishment for our sin.

Question 2. God's discipline proves that we are his children. In the immediate moment, discipline may feel like punishment, but the aim is different. Punishment looks backward and focuses on making the offender pay; discipline looks forward and focuses on shaping the person's character.

Question 3. Ideally all parental discipline is motivated by love for the child. Some participants may have experienced unduly harsh or unfair discipline from parents or other authority figures. Stay focused on the fact that God disciplines only with loving purposes for our good.

Questions 5 and 6. When we go through difficulties, is God disciplining us, or are our troubles only the natural result of living in a fallen world? The question is legitimate and cannot always be answered in the immediate moment. In any case, we should take a look at our behavior and attitudes in the light of Scripture, asking, "Is God getting my attention and showing me where I'm off track?" That is an excellent prayer to directly ask the Lord and expect his answer in due time.

STUDY 5. GRATEFUL FOR GOD'S GRACE. EPHESIANS 1:3-14.

PURPOSE: To grow in appreciation of God's mercy toward us in Christ.

General note. The words "in Ephesus" (v. 1) do not appear in some Greek manuscripts. This letter may have been a general letter intended to be passed among several churches.

Question 5. Paul uses the phrase "in the heavenly realms" five times in this letter: Ephesians 1:3, 1:20, 2:6, 3:10, and 6:12. Our faith does not merely help us cope with life or feel better here and now. Paul is confident that Christ is already reigning in heaven and has secured our place with him there.

Question 7. If we imagine that we can merit God's favor through our own righteousness, we cannot possibly be grateful for "redemption through his blood, the forgiveness of sins" and "the riches of God's grace that he lavished on us." We must realize that we are the undeserving recipients of these gifts.

Question 8. Participants will name various things depending on their personal experience: strained relationships in families and marriages, racial or class animosity, political bickering, international conflict, physical and mental disabilities, longstanding grudges affecting generations. Our fallen world affords unlimited manifestations of brokenness.

STUDY 6. GLAD TO TAKE HEAT. 1 PETER 4:12-19.

PURPOSE: To find joy in enduring persecution for Christ.

Question 1. People's common expectation is that wrongdoers, not the innocent, should suffer. This passage mirrors Peter's remarkable words earlier in his letter that "it is better, if it is God's will, to suffer for doing good than for doing evil" (1 Peter 3:17).

Question 2. If we mistakenly believe that faith in Christ will protect us from adversity, then suffering of any kind will come as a shock. The "fiery ordeal" (v. 12) facing these believers is undoubtedly persecution for their faith, which Peter earlier compared to gold tested and refined by fire (1 Peter 1:6-7). They have been scattered throughout Asia Minor (1:1) and are being slandered by enemies (3:15-16).

Question 4. Peter knew what he was talking about. From the beginning of the church, he had experienced suffering for Christ. In Jerusalem he and the other apostles were arrested, put in jail, miraculously released, brought before the Jewish council, ordered not to preach in the name of Jesus, flogged, and then let go. Acts 5:41 records, "The apostles left the Sanhedrin, rejoicing because they had been counted worthy of suffering disgrace for the Name."

Question 7. "Believers experience the judgment of earthly courts (1 Peter 4:6), but Peter probably sees that suffering also as God's discipline, as Jewish teachers did. Throughout history, persecution has refined and strengthened the church" (Craig S. Keener, *The IVP Bible Background Commentary: New Testament* [Downers Grove, IL: InterVarsity Press, 1993], 720). God's judgment on believers "is based on grace, for we never hear of God judging Christians for sins that they have repented of. Yet, gracious as it is, such a judgment is very real and very painful, a point upon which all of the New Testament authors agree" (Walter C. Kaiser Jr., Peter H. Davids, F. F. Bruce, and Manfred T.

Brauch, *Hard Sayings of the Bible* [Downers Grove, IL: InterVarsity Press, 1996], 722).

STUDY 7. INTO THE UNKNOWN WITH GRATITUDE. 2 CHRONICLES 20:1-30.

PURPOSE: To face an unknown future with confidence in God and thankfulness for what he will accomplish for his glory and your good.

Question 1. Notice that both the king and the people immediately sought the Lord. They did not first turn to idols or perform pagan rituals and then turn to God as a last resort. Fasting is connected with the urgency of prayer, when appealing to God becomes even more important than food. For other biblical examples of fasting and prayer, see 1 Samuel 7:2-6 (when the ark of the covenant was returned from the Philistines); Ezra 8:21-23 (for a safe journey back from Babylon); Nehemiah 1:4 (when Nehemiah heard that Jerusalem was in ruins); Esther 4:15-16 (implied prayer before Esther petitioned the king to save the Jews); Jeremiah 36:4-10 (when Jerusalem was besieged); Daniel 9:1-3 (during the exile to Babylon); Jonah 3:5-10 (the Ninevites' response to Jonah's preaching); Acts 9:8-19 (Saul's conversion); Acts 13:1-3 (when Barnabas and Saul were set apart for gospel travels). The Gospels of Matthew and Luke record Jesus' forty-day fast after his baptism.

Question 3. Jehoshaphat appeals to God's long history with his people, going back before they were divided into the two kingdoms of Israel and Judah. He acknowledges that his own kingdom of Judah would not even exist if God had not enabled their ancestors to conquer the land's previous inhabitants.

Question 6. Jahaziel's prophecy places full confidence in the Lord to deliver the people from the enemy. Acting as an inspired "spy," he gives specifics of the enemy's movements. The Jews will not even have to fight the battle. The Lord will do the fighting and will win the victory on their behalf.

Question 7. As they go, they might reasonably be calling out variations of "Lord, help us!" "Defeat the enemy!" "Don't let us turn back in panic!" "Go with us into the battle!" "Give us victory!" Instead, they are already thanking God for his enduring love.

STUDY 8. UNENDING THANKS. PSALM 107.

PURPOSE: To maintain an attitude of thankfulness to God that does not fade after a crisis is over.

Question 2. There are similarities here with Israel's exodus from Egypt. The Israelites cried out to the Lord for deliverance from slavery, and he answered them (Exodus 2:23-25). Because they lost faith in the Lord (Numbers 14), they wandered in the desert for forty years and at times experienced hunger and thirst. However, the wanderings of Psalm 107 appear more random than those of the exodus, where the Israelites were fed by the Lord and led by his pillar of cloud. There is also no indication that they were finally led into the promised land because they "cried out to the LORD in their trouble"; God simply announced that it was time (Joshua 1:1-2).

Question 4. While the Israelites' bondage in Egypt was not because of sin, their exile to Babylon was the direct result of rebellion against God (2 Chronicles 36:15-17). Psalm 107 may have been written after Israel returned from Babylon; verse 16 is almost identical to God's promise of the return (Isaiah 45:2). Bronze and iron (vv. 10, 16) were the strongest possible materials at the time. The prophet Jeremiah asked rhetorically, "Can a man break iron—iron from the north—or bronze?" (Jeremiah 15:12).

Question 5. Some examples of things that can imprison people, including Christians, are emotional disturbances, warped ideas about God, addiction to drugs or alcohol, pornography, excessive self-indulgence, exaggerated pride, and destructive relationships.

Question 6. If these fools' illness was the result of rebellion against the Lord, then repenting and obeying his "word" (his will revealed in his commandments) could restore them onto the path to health.

Question 7. We do not think of Israel as a seafaring nation, but they did pursue trade by ship on the Mediterranean Sea and Red Sea (1 Kings 9:26-28; 10:22). At the same time, the sea was regarded with fear and associated with ungodly chaos. Scripture shows God's power to both cause and calm storms on water—for example, Jonah on the Mediterranean (Jonah 1:4-16) and Jesus on the Sea of Galilee (Mark 4:35-41). Both events revealed God's power over nature and resulted in awe and worship.

Dale and Sandy Larsen have written more than forty books and Bible studies together, including Growing Older & Wiser *in the LifeGuide Bible Studies series. They live in Rochester, Minnesota.*

WHAT SHOULD WE STUDY NEXT?

LifeGuide® BIBLE STUDIES

Since 1985 LifeGuide® Bible Studies have provided solid inductive Bible study content with field-tested questions that get groups talking—making for a one-of-a-kind Bible study experience. This series has more than 120 titles on Old and New Testament books, character studies, and topical studies. IVP's LifeGuide Finder is a great tool for searching for your next study topic: https://ivpress.com/lifeguidefinder.

Here are some ideas to get you started.

BIBLE BOOKS

An in-depth study of a Bible book is one of the richest experiences you could have in opening up the riches of Scripture. Many groups begin with a Gospel such as Mark or John. These guides are divided into two parts so that if twenty or twenty-six weeks feels like too much to do at once, the group can feel free to do half of the studies and take a break with another topic.

A shorter letter such as Philippians or Ephesians is also a great way to start. Shorter Old Testament studies include Ruth, Esther, and Job.

TOPICAL SERIES

Here are a few ideas of short series you might put together to cover a year of curriculum on a theme.

Christian Formation: *Christian Beliefs* (12 studies by Stephen D. Eyre), *Christian Character* (12 studies by Andrea Sterk & Peter Scazzero), *Christian Disciplines* (12 studies by Andrea Sterk & Peter Scazzero), *Evangelism* (12 studies by Rebecca Pippert & Ruth Siemens).

Building Community: *Christian Community* (10 studies by Rob Suggs), *Friendship* (10 studies by Carolyn Nystrom), *Spiritual Gifts* (8 studies by R. Paul Stevens), *Loving Justice* (12 studies by Bob and Carol Hunter).

GUIDES FOR SPECIFIC TYPES OF GROUPS

If you have a group that is serving a particular demographic, here are some specific ideas. Also note the list of studies for seekers on the back cover.

Women's Groups: *Women of the New Testament, Women of the Old Testament, Woman of God, Women & Identity, Motherhood*

Marriage and Parenting: *Marriage, Parenting, Grandparenting*